Witchcraft

COLORING BOOK
FOR ADULTS

NOURISH THE SPIRIT AND
CHANNEL CREATIVE ENERGY

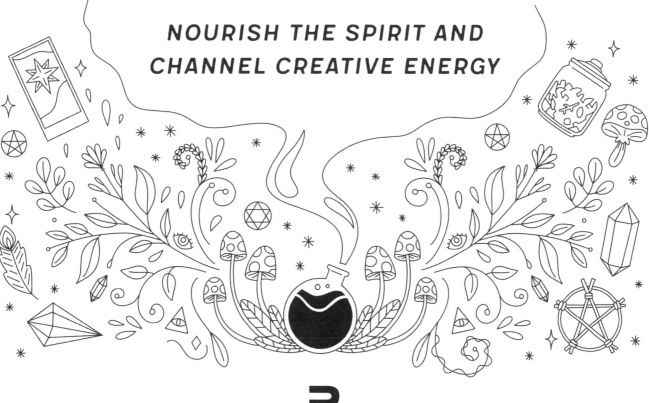

ROCKRIDGE
PRESS

For general information on our other products and services or to obtain technical support, please contact our Customer Care Department within the United States at (866) 744-2665, or outside the United States at (510) 253-0500.

Rockridge Press publishes its books in a variety of electronic and print formats. Some content that appears in print may not be available in electronic books, and vice versa.

TRADEMARKS: Rockridge Press and the Rockridge Press logo are trademarks or registered trademarks of Callisto Media Inc. and/or its affiliates, in the United States and other countries, and may not be used without written permission. All other trademarks are the property of their respective owners. Rockridge Press is not associated with any product or vendor mentioned in this book.

Interior and Cover Designer: Linda Snorina
Art Producer: Sara Feinstein
Editor: Kelly Koester
Production Editor: Jael Fogle
Production Manager: Riley Hoffman

Illustrations © 2021 Collaborate Agency

Paperback ISBN: 978-1-63807-778-7
R0

Printed in Canada

THE POWER OF WITCHCRAFT

A witch, by modern definition, is anyone who practices witchcraft. Witchcraft is not a religion. It is a craft—something that we do with our hands, our minds, and our energy. Witchcraft is an empowering practice that any person can learn, cultivate, and personalize. It is all about stepping outside of our mundane world and choosing to take on a perspective of mysticism and reverence for nature, life, and the energetic forces of this world. But what makes witchcraft so powerful is that it's not just about what we can see; it's about everything in between. It's about appreciating the world around us. It is the love for spirits, messages, otherworldliness, unexplainable things, mysterious connections, and the universal system of checks and balances. That is witchcraft. Witchcraft is about taking the raw, beautiful, and powerful forces of our world and using them to create change.

HOW WITCHCRAFT EMBRACES SELF-CARE

Witchcraft is the tool that allows you to be the conductor of the symphony of magic that is your life. A major aspect of being a witch involves working with the inner parts of ourselves and our intuition. Our magic is an extension of our being, which is why it intersects perfectly with self-care. By tapping into the healing nature of witchcraft through self-reflection, creativity, and mindfulness, we can actively engage in the magical maintenance of the self.

Just like witchcraft, talk of self-care seems to be everywhere these days. And as with witchcraft, it is a very personal practice that differs from person to person. To some of us, it is a warm bubble bath with rose petals, a bottle of wine, an indulgent meal, or a vacation. But at its core, self-care is less about the material means of modern luxury and more about the actions and the conscious effort to care for ourselves. These actions can be taking 15 to 30 minutes of the day to meditate, saying no when we have reached our capacity of doing for others, or creating boundaries to protect our personal needs.

Coloring is an excellent way to practice both witchcraft and self-care. The act of coloring not only helps you channel your creativity and self-expression, it also helps you refocus attention, ease anxiety, and achieve more mindfulness. This in turn helps you open up channels for positivity and connection in other areas of your life.

A WITCH'S GUIDE TO COLOR

Produced by wavelengths of light, color electrifies our senses with various psychological and spiritual effects. The natural world is rich with color, and we have learned that color can have meaning, like the three colors of stoplights. Even our bodies emit colors around us, called auras, which manifest differently depending on one's mental, physical, and spiritual state. Using color in magic can be done by selecting certain colored candles for a spell, different crystals, clothing, jewelry, paper, etc. As you dive into these coloring pages, bring intentionality to your color craft by being aware of colors and their correspondences.

RED: passion, strength, and courage

PINK: friendship, joy, and beauty

ORANGE: energy, enthusiasm, and confidence

YELLOW: communication, imagination, and inspiration

GREEN: prosperity, health, and fertility

BLUE: calm, peace, and serenity

PURPLE: wisdom, intuition, and mysticism

BROWN: stability, comfort, and foundation

BLACK: banishing, protection, and absorption

WHITE: purity, spirituality, and deflection

GRAY: balance, neutralization, and judgment

SILVER: lunar energy, glamour, and mystery

GOLD: solar energy, success, and wishes

A DEDICATION RITUAL TO SELF-CARE

Let's kick off our magical self-care journey with a self-dedication ritual. This will help further align our minds with the magic of moving ourselves forward.

MATERIALS

Knife

1 white pillar candle

Lighter or matches

1 piece of paper

Pen

Cauldron or fireproof bowl

1 fresh white rose

Camera or smartphone

1. Use the knife to carve your name into the candle, along with any other sigils or personal symbols of power that connect to you. Lick your thumb and slide it over your carved name to seal it with your essence.

2. Light the candle and write what you pledge to achieve in the next 90 days on a piece of paper by candlelight. It can be as long or as simple as you like, but it should be personal and straight from your heart.

3. Light the paper with the flame from the candle and place it into your cauldron or fireproof bowl.

4. Say aloud: "I dedicate myself to unlocking the magic within me. I conjure self-love, so mote it be."

5. Remove each petal from the rose, then drop them into the pot of ashes while thinking about how amazing it feels to tend to your needs.

6. Blow out the candle flame and take the pot outside. Sprinkle the mixture of ashes and petals on the earth. Take a photo of yourself to document your dedication.

7. Each day, relight your candle until it is burnt out. Save any remains from your candle in a safe place to be used in a future spell.

THE SUN

ACE OF CUPS

THE TOWER

THE EMPRESS

WHEEL OF FORTUNE